Animal
Look-Alikes

By Rachel Griffiths and Margaret Clyne

CELEBRATION PRESS
Pearson Learning Group

Contents

Introduction

Is it a frog or a toad? Is it a moth or a butterfly? Sometimes it is hard to tell. Some animals look alike. They may even act alike. Different animals are never exactly the same, though. This book will help you learn to tell the differences between some animals that look alike. So read on and take a closer look.

Butterflies and Moths

Butterflies and moths are alike in some ways. They are both **insects**. Both have wings and antennae. Both usually feed on plant nectar.

butterfly ▼

antennae

wings

▼ moth

wings

antennae

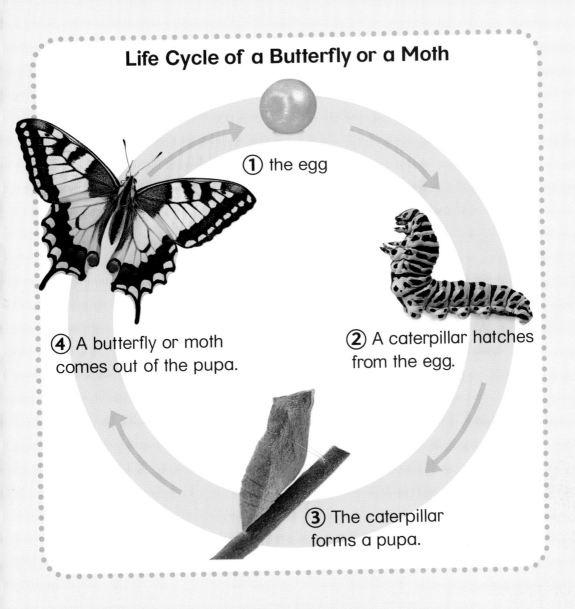

Life Cycle of a Butterfly or a Moth

① the egg

② A caterpillar hatches from the egg.

③ The caterpillar forms a pupa.

④ A butterfly or moth comes out of the pupa.

Butterflies and moths also have similar **life cycles**. They both lay eggs and spend part of their lives as caterpillars. Are butterflies and moths exactly alike? Turn the page to find out!

Butterflies and moths are not the same. Most moths have wide, fuzzy bodies. Butterflies have thinner bodies that are not fuzzy.

Butterflies have knobs on the ends of their antennae. Moths do not. Many moth antennae look like feathers.

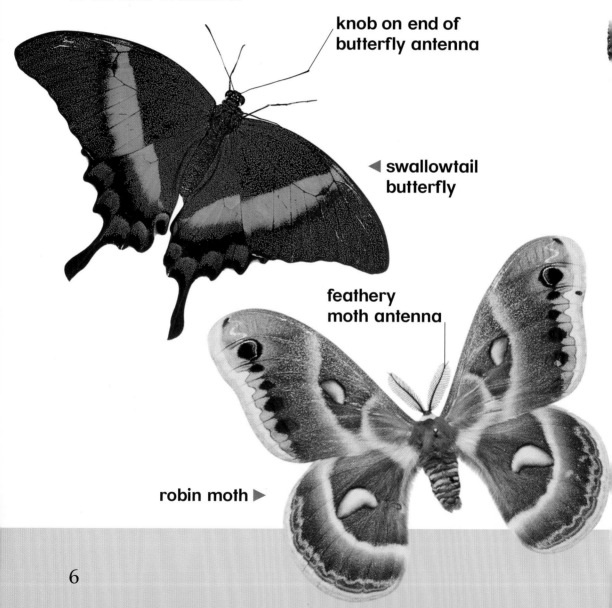

knob on end of butterfly antenna

◀ swallowtail butterfly

feathery moth antenna

robin moth ▶

◀ puss moth

▲ comma butterfly

It is hard to see this moth because it is almost the same color as the tree bark.

▲ acacia carpenter moth

▲ Cleopatra butterfly

Butterflies are usually more colorful than moths. Moths are often brown or gray. These dull colors help moths hide. This is called **camouflage**.

Alligators and Crocodiles

Alligators and crocodiles are another pair of animal look-alikes. They both have bumpy skin, short legs, and long, strong tails. They are both **reptiles**.

▼ crocodile

▼ alligator

Alligators and crocodiles are both good swimmers. They both have very sharp teeth, and both will eat any kind of animal they can catch. Are alligators and crocodiles exactly alike? Turn the page to find out!

crocodile
snout

alligator
snout

Up close, the snouts on alligators and crocodiles look very different. Alligators have rounded snouts. Crocodile snouts are more pointed.

Alligators and crocodiles have different jaws, too. When an alligator closes its mouth, most of its teeth are hidden. Crocodile teeth stick out of their closed mouths. They make it look like the crocodile is smiling.

Is it an alligator or a crocodile?

Places Where Alligators and Crocodiles Live

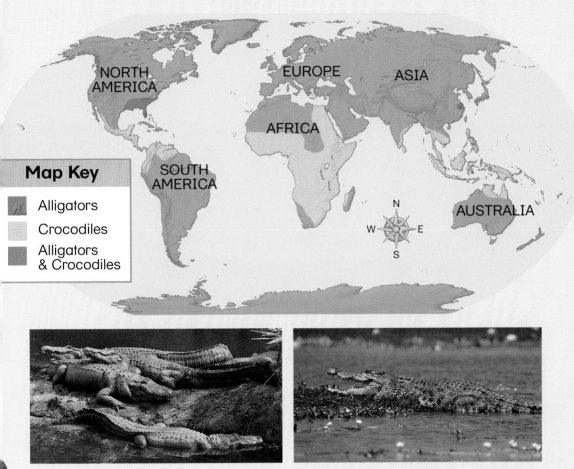

Map Key
- Alligators
- Crocodiles
- Alligators & Crocodiles

NORTH AMERICA

EUROPE

ASIA

AFRICA

SOUTH AMERICA

AUSTRALIA

Many North American alligators live in Florida.

Crocodiles live in the Northern Territory of Australia.

Alligators and crocodiles are found around the world. Alligators live only in the United States and China. Crocodiles live in North America and Asia, too, and in South America, Africa, and Australia.

Frogs and Toads

It's hard to tell the difference between frogs and toads. They both have four legs and can have green or brown skin. They both have eyes that stick out, and both eat insects. They are **amphibians**.

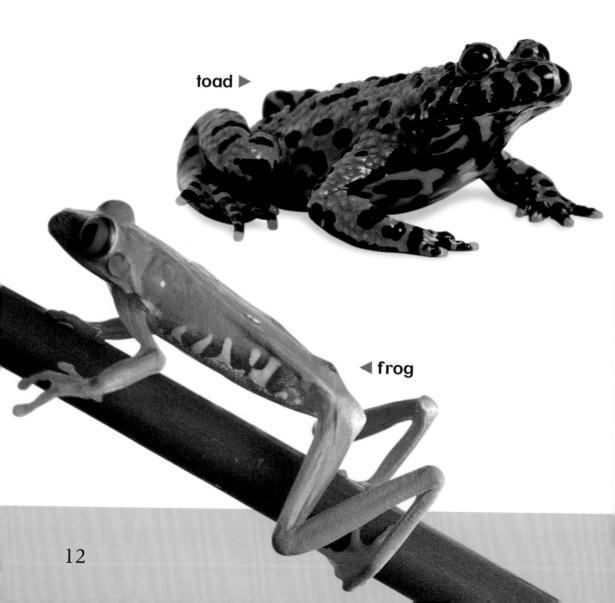

toad ▶

◀ frog

Life Cycle of a Frog or a Toad

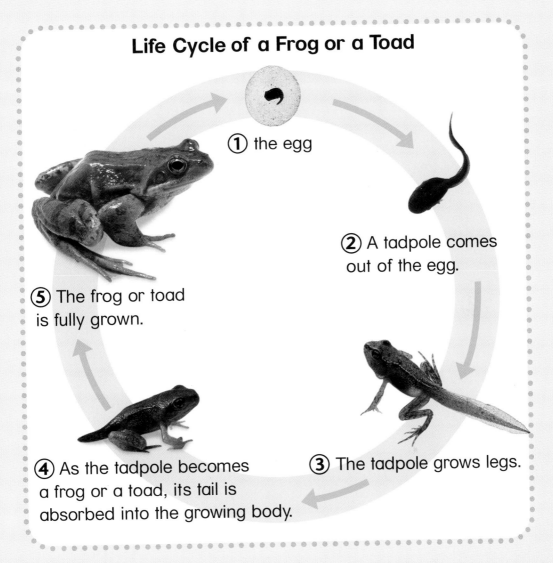

① the egg

② A tadpole comes out of the egg.

③ The tadpole grows legs.

④ As the tadpole becomes a frog or a toad, its tail is absorbed into the growing body.

⑤ The frog or toad is fully grown.

Frogs and toads also have similar life cycles. They both start out as eggs. Then they hatch into tadpoles and live under water. Finally, they become adults and hop onto land. Are frogs and toads exactly alike? Turn the page to find out!

Frogs and toads look different. Frogs have skin that is smooth and wet. Toads have skin that is bumpy and dry. Toads usually have wider bodies than frogs, too.

▼ toad

bumpy, dry skin

Frogs and toads usually live in different **environments**. Many frogs spend a lot of time in or near the water. Toads live mostly on land.

smooth, wet skin

▼ frog

Seals and Sea Lions

Seals and sea lions are hard to tell apart. Both have sleek fur and flippers that they use to move quickly in water. They are **mammals**.

▲ seals

Sea lions and seals live in the ocean. They are great swimmers and divers. Both catch their food as they swim.

Sea lions and seals both climb onto land to rest and to have their babies. Are sea lions and seals exactly alike? Turn the page to find out!

sea lions ▼

Sea lions are bigger than seals. They are also noisier. One of their nicknames is "sea dogs" because they make loud barking sounds. Seals make softer, grunting sounds.

Both animals have good hearing. However, seals have tiny ear holes, while sea lions have ear flaps on the sides of their heads.

ear flap

hind flippers

▼ **sea lion**

hind flippers

The ways seals and sea lions move on land are very different. Sea lions pull their hind flippers forward and move using all four flippers. The hind flippers on seals don't move that way. Seals scoot along on their stomachs.

ear hole

▼ seal

A seal moves on its stomach.

A sea lion holds its body up
when it uses its flippers to move.

Look-Alikes Everywhere

Animal look-alikes are everywhere. They come in all shapes and sizes. Some are insects, some are mammals, some are reptiles, and some are amphibians.

Up close, however, animal look-alikes are not always as alike as they seem. Their differences can be great or small. These differences are what make each animal unique.

▲ leopard

▲ cheetah

Other Animal Look-Alikes

rabbit

hare

turtle

tortoise

hedgehog

echidna

coyote

wolf

Recommended Reading

Learn more about animals that look alike by reading the materials listed below.

Books:

What's the Difference?: 10 Animal Look-Alikes
by Judy Diehl, David Plumb, and Vlasta van Kampen (Illustrator)
Annick Press, September, 2000

Eyewitness Explorers: Mammals
by David Burnie and Deni Brown
Dorling Kindersley, March, 1998

Crocodiles & Alligators
by Seymour Simon
Harper Collins, August, 2001

Web Sites:

National Geographic Kids site:
www.nationalgeographic.com/kids/

Children's Smithsonian Institute:
www.si.edu/kids/

Friends of the National Zoo:
www.nationalzoo.si.edu/

Glossary

amphibians   kinds of animals that can live on land and in water

camouflage   the color or shape of an animal that helps it hide

environments   the conditions in an area including the variety of living things, the type of land, and the climate

insects   kinds of animals that have three body parts and six legs

life cycles   all the changes animals or plants go through as they develop

mammals   animals that are fed with their mother's milk; mammals have fur or hair

reptiles   kinds of coldblooded animals that often have scales and lay eggs

Index

tree frog

tree toad